COPING WITH FEELINGS WORKBOOK

For Adults in Recovery from Chemical Dependency

Dennis C. Daley

LP **LEARNING PUBLICATIONS, INC.**
Holmes Beach, Florida

ISBN 1-55691-108-4

Learning Publications, Inc.
P.O. Box 1338
5351 Gulf Drive
Holmes Beach, FL 34218-1338

Printing: 5 4 3 2 1   Year: 10 9 8 7 6

Printed in the United States of America.

CONTENTS

ACKNOWLEDGMENTS

Thanks to Cindy Hurney for her creative abilities in designing the format of this workbook and for her excellent word processing skills.

DEDICATION

To Kenny and Edna Crooks for sharing much love, fun, and humor with my family.

ABOUT THE AUTHOR

Dennis C. Daley is assistant professor of psychiatry and director of the Center for Psychiatric and Chemical Dependency Services for the University of Pittsburgh Medical Center at the Western Psychiatric Institute and Clinic. He has been involved in developing treatment services for clients and families for many years in both mental health and chemical dependency treatment settings. Mr. Daley has written over 30 books and workbooks on recovery from chemical dependency, psychiatric illness or combined disorders, and relapse prevention. He is also involved in several research projects funded by the National Institute of Drug Abuse and Mr. Daley lectures throughout the United States and Canada. Mr. Daley has developed over 25 recovery oriented educational videos including the *Living Sober* series, for individuals recovering from substance abuse, and the *Promise of Recovery* series, for individuals recovering from mental health disorders.

Introduction

Recovery from chemical dependency requires you to look at many different areas of your life — it goes beyond simply stopping your use of alcohol or drugs. While abstinence is very important, so is change. Change involves learning new information, increasing your self-awareness, and developing new skills for coping with problems.

Recovery provides you with an opportunity to make changes within yourself and in your lifestyle. As a result, it gives you a chance to grow, to become a better person and more fulfilled in your life. The opportunity for self-improvement is one of the many benefits of recovery.

This recovery workbook was written to help you better understand and cope with your feelings or emotions and can be used by anyone with a chemical dependency, including those who have another addictive disorder (compulsive gambling, compulsive sex, compulsive eating, etc.) or a psychiatric illness (depressive disorder, anxiety disorder, personality disorder, etc.).

You do not have to complete every section of this workbook. The sections and tasks that you complete should depend on which of the various emotions you believe you need to deal with as part of your recovery. This workbook can be used whether you are just starting your recovery journey or you have been in recovery for months or longer.

Recovery requires hard work and a commitment to change, and this workbook requires you to take a *proactive* approach. It contains a number of recovery tasks aimed at helping you deal with specific feelings. You will be asked to do a lot of thinking and self-reflection, answer questions to figure out what your problems are with your feelings, and determine the changes you want to make.

To change, you have to set goals for recovery, develop a plan of action, and take specific steps to reach your goals. It is helpful to put your plan in writing.

You are advised to discuss your completed workbook activities with a therapist, counselor, sponsor, or another person in recovery. If you are in an inpatient rehabilitation program or dual-disorders program, you can discuss your answers to sections of this workbook with one or more members of your treatment team.

As you complete the workbook, you will discover that some of the sections and tasks can be applied to different problems or recovery issues you are dealing with. For example, the connection between your beliefs and thoughts (cognitive), how you feel (emotional), and how you act (behavioral) is emphasized whether you are dealing with feelings such as anger, depression, or guilt. You will also discover that this workbook can help you with issues that may have little or nothing to do with your chemical dependency. You will learn a variety of coping strategies that may be used across a range of problems.

OVERVIEW OF WORKBOOK

The first two sections of this workbook focus on the importance of recognizing feelings and provide an eight-step process that can be used to cope with feelings. The following six sections focus on understanding and coping with specific feelings such as anger, anxiety and worry, boredom, depression, emptiness and joylessness, guilt and shame. The last two sections focus on expressing love and other positive feelings.

The appendices include a *Coping with Feelings Worksheet* as well as a list of *Suggested Readings.* You can learn more about the topics in this workbook by reading other books, workbooks, and recovery materials.

SOME SUGGESTIONS ON HOW TO USE THIS WORKBOOK

There are many ways in which you can use this workbook to help your recovery and your personal growth. Your attitude and approach is very important and you can get the most out of this workbook by:

■ **Being honest**

Complete the questions as honestly as you can even if you have negative attitudes or thoughts or don't feel like answering.

■ **Being patient**

There are no short-cuts, easy answers, or quick ways to deal with your problems. Change takes time and you can't hurry it along.

■ **Making a long-term commitment**

Recovery requires you to make a long-term commitment to change. Changes seldom occur in the short-run. Making a long-term commitment helps you hang in there during difficult times when you are struggling or find yourself not wanting to change.

■ **Being self-reflective**

Think seriously about what you read and how you respond to the questions. Self-reflection helps you figure out where you are now and what you need to change.

■ **Being realistic**

Don't try to set goals that are too high or can't be reached.

■ **Working hard**

Don't try to slide through recovery. Hard work usually pays off great dividends and is worth the effort, especially when you are struggling with problems.

■ **Setting goals for change**

You are much more likely to work a recovery plan if you identify things you want to change and set goals. Setting goals gives you something to work towards.

■ **Using 12-step programs and other support groups**

Programs such as Alcoholics Anonymous (AA), Narcotics Anonymous (NA), and Cocaine Anonymous (CA) provide an excellent way to deal with chemical dependency. Attend meetings, get a "sponsor," read program recovery literature, and learn the "tools," especially the 12-step programs.

■ **Sharing your plan and goals with others**

Don't try to recover alone. Lean on others and talk about your problems, concerns, questions, frustrations, and feelings. Others can give you support, advice, and feedback on your recovery plan.

■ **Using professional treatment**

Professional treatment can be sought by contacting a local drug and alcohol clinic or private therapist. Some people need to get detoxified in a hospital or enter a rehabilitation program in order to get clean.

■ **Allowing room for mistakes**

Everyone makes mistakes, especially when trying something new. Changing any area of your life is trying something new so expect to make some mistakes. Try to learn from your mistakes.

■ Taking a look at your progress

It helps to regularly review your recovery. At first you may wish to check your progress each day or week. This allows you to assess progress and obstacles in your recovery.

■ Rewarding your progress

Do something nice for yourself as a way of rewarding progress that you make towards your goals. Don't take your hard work for granted.

1
Recognizing Emotions or Feelings

One of the common tasks of recovery is coping with emotions or feelings which reduces your chances of relapse improving your mental health and your ability to get along with others.

Many alcoholics and drug addicts talk about their emotional growth being stunted because of their addiction. Alcohol and drugs can cover up your feelings, exaggerate them, or cause you to express them in ways that aren't healthy.

Sometimes emotions or feelings are referred to as "positive" or "negative." Positive emotions include feeling cheerful, excited, glad, hopeful, loving, or thankful. These usually make you feel good. Negative emotions include feeling angry, bitter, disappointed, jealous, or humiliated. These usually make you feel bad or uncomfortable.

However, be careful about labeling feelings as only positive or negative. A particular emotion and how you deal with it can become a negative or a positive experience. Excitement, for example, can be negative if it leads to reckless or impulsive behavior or making poor decisions. Or, it can be positive and make you feel energized and invested in what you are doing. Anger can be negative and drag you down, making you feel upset and revengeful because you feel others are treating you unjustly. Or, anger can be used in positive ways. Anger is energy that can empower and motivate you to resolve problems, conflicts, or work harder towards a goal that you wish to achieve.

There are a variety of feelings that may be experienced. Use this list to help guide you in answering the questions that follow. Remember, this list is not all inclusive as there are other feelings you may experience. These are some of the more common ones.

Affection	Afraid	Anger	Anxious
Ashamed	Bitter	Bored	Caring
Cheerful	Depressed	Delighted	Disappointed
Distrustful	Eager	Embarrassed	Empty
Fearful	Forgiving	Friendly	Glad
Grateful	Guilty	Happy	Hateful
Hopeful	Hopeless	Hostile	Humble
Humiliated	Humorous	Impatient	Irritated

Jealous	Joyful	Joyless	Lonely
Loving	Miserable	Passion	Panicky
Pessimistic	Playful	Proud	Rejected
Relaxed	Remorseful	Resentful	Sad
Secure	Sexy	Shy	Sympathetic
Tender	Terrified	Thankful	Threatened
Uptight	Useful	Useless	Wonderful
Worried	Worthwhile		

The following questions will help you assess how you experience and deal with your feelings.

1. Are there certain feelings or emotions that you seem to experience more than others? If yes, which ones?

_____

_____

_____

2. Are there feelings that you tend to avoid or find very uncomfortable? If yes, which ones?

_____

_____

_____

3. Are you mainly aware of, or apt to express, only your negative feelings? If so, why?

_____

_____

_____

4. Are you mainly aware of, or apt to express, only your positive feelings? If so, why?

_____

_____

_____

_____

5. Which feelings make you feel the most vulnerable to relapse to alcohol or drug use?

_____

_____

_____

_____

2
Steps for Coping With Feelings

Understanding and coping with feelings reduces your chances of relapse. Following are steps you can take to help you cope with feelings or emotional states. You can use these steps regardless of the specific emotion you are dealing with. In later sections, additional information will be provided in relation to some of the more common emotions (anger, boredom, depression, guilt, etc.) that can complicate recovery.

■ Step 1: Recognize and label your feelings

Don't deny your feelings because this can cause you more difficulty in the long run. Even if you feel what you believe is a "negative" or "bad" feeling, remember that it is simply an honest feeling. Feeling an emotion doesn't mean you have to "act" on it.

You can also look for "patterns" in regard to your feelings. Do you tend to experience certain feelings much more frequently than others? Does your response to certain situations or events form a pattern? For example, are you prone to feeling anxious and worried when you are faced with a difficult task where others put demands on you? Are you prone to feeling sad and depressed after receiving criticism from others?

You may find it helpful to keep a written journal or use worksheets to identify your feelings.

■ Step 2: Be aware of how your feelings show

Pay attention to how your feelings show in your body language, physical symptoms, thoughts, and your behavior. Use these various clues to raise awareness of your feelings.

For example, pacing and feeling "keyed up" or tight may indicate one person is angry. For another, it may indicate feeling worried. A person may be prone to headaches or other physical complaints when upset and angry. These, or other physical cues, may be a sign that something is going on that needs your attention.

When feeling upset, rejected, or frustrated, one person may be prone to going on mini shopping sprees. Another may turn to food and eat too much, or turn to alcohol or drugs. Another person may withdraw and avoid others when upset. The ways in which feelings show through behavior are endless.

■ **Step 3: Look for causes of your feelings**

Feelings aren't usually "caused" by other people or events but by how you think about these. Your beliefs about feelings play a big role in how you deal with them. For example, if you believe anger is bad and not to be expressed, you are likely to deny angry feelings or hold them inside.

To understand why you feel the way you do, look at the connection between what you believe or think, how you feel, and how you act. Any of these components can affect the other.

■ **Step 4: Evaluate the effects of your feelings and your coping style, both on yourself and other people**

How is your physical or mental health affected by your feelings and how you express them? How is your behavior or self-esteem affected? How are your relationships influenced? If your emotions or the ways in which you cope with them cause you distress or problems in your relationships, then you need to work hard on changing how you deal with them.

You need to consider how your feelings affect other people. For example, if you are depressed or angry, how does this impact your family?

There may be many positive effects of your emotions and how you cope with them. Most likely, there are some feelings that have more of a positive effect on your life and some that have more of a negative effect. If a feeling or how you deal with it causes problems for you, this is a signal that you should change how you cope with it.

■ **Step 5: Identify coping strategies to deal with your feelings**

You can continue to use old coping methods if they are effective. Or, if needed, you can learn new coping methods. There is no right way to cope with your feelings. How you cope depends on the specific situation at hand. Having a variety of coping strategies puts you in a good position to effectively deal with your feelings. Coping strategies include verbal (what you say), cognitive (how you think), and behavioral (how you act).

Problems with feelings are sometimes related to a mood disorder. Serious mood disturbances associated with psychiatric illness may require medications. For example, antidepressant medications help with some types of depressive illness. Lithium or anticonvulsant medications help with bipolar illness. Severe feelings of anxiety or panic may also require medication. Medication should be used in conjunction with therapy or other coping strategies mentioned above. Medications used to treat symptoms of a serious mood disorder should not be viewed in the same light as using alcohol or other drugs in order to get high. Alcoholics and drug addicts are not immune to psychiatric disorders and some require medication in addition to therapy.

■ Step 6: Rehearse or practice new coping strategies

Practicing ahead of time how you might deal with a particular feeling, especially when another person is involved, can make you feel more prepared and confident of what you will say. Learning to express feelings is a skill that has to be *learned and practiced* just like any other skill.

Sometimes you can practice alone by thinking of different things that you can say in certain situations. You can even practice talking out loud how you might deal with your feelings towards another person in a given situation.

Or, you can practice with another person. For example, if you feel very attracted to a person you work with and want to ask this person out on a date, but feel uncomfortable doing so, you can practice with a friend or family member.

■ Step 7: Put your new coping strategies into action

You can come up with a wonderful plan to deal with feelings but if you don't put it into action, it does you little good. Action is needed for change. You have to translate your desire or need to change into your actual behavior.

Don't worry about making a mistake as this is to be expected when you first change how you cope with your feelings.

■ Step 8: Change your coping strategies based on your evaluation of their effectiveness

All strategies will not work the same in all situations. The key is having several coping strategies to rely on so that you don't use the same strategy all of the time.

Even if a coping strategy works well in one situation, it may not work in another. Make sure you have several strategies that you can rely upon to help you cope with your feelings.

3
Anger

Anger contributes to alcohol and drug abuse as well as relapse. Much friction can be caused in a relationship if you ignore your anger or act on it in ways that hurt other people physically or emotionally.

On the other hand, anger is an emotion that can empower you if dealt with in a positive way. Anger can motivate you to set or reach goals or work hard to accomplish things in your life.

Anger, in itself, doesn't cause problems. How you think about and express it determines how anger affects your life.

Some people try to ignore their anger and hold it inside — they stew on the inside and become depressed. They may let anger out by dragging their feet, criticizing others behind their backs, or avoiding people.

Others let their anger out too quickly. They lash out at others, yell, cuss, scream, or act in other hostile ways. Some get into fights or show other forms of physical violence towards other people. Some destroy objects or property.

The questions that follow will help you see where you stand in relation to anger and how you express it.

1. On a scale of one to 10, how much of a problem is your anger or how you cope with it or express it (✓ your rating)?

1	3	5	7	10
No Problem	Moderate Problem	Significant Problem	Serious Problem	Severe Problem
_____	_____	_____	_____	_____

2. My anger shows in the following ways (e.g., I get sad, frustrated, pace, feel nervous, etc.):

_____

_____

_____

3. I usually deal with anger by (e.g., holding it inside, letting it out immediately, talking it out, lashing out at others, fighting, etc.):

_____

_____

_____

4. I learned the following from my parents about anger and how to express it:

_____

_____

_____

5. My anger affects me in the following ways:

_____

_____

_____

6. My anger affects my relationships in the following ways:

_____

_____

_____

7. My anger affects my use of alcohol or other drugs by:

_____

_____

_____

_____

8. I am still very angry at the following people:

_____

_____

_____

9. I can use my anger in a positive way by:

_____

_____

_____

_____

ANGER BUSTERS

- **Recognize your angry feelings**

Pay attention to body cues, thoughts, and behaviors which tell you're angry. Use your anger cues to admit that you are angry. Don't deny, hide, minimize, or ignore your anger.

- **Figure out why you are angry**

When you feel angry figure out of where it is coming from. Does it relate to something another person did or said to you? Does it relate to an event, experience, or situation? Or, is your anger caused by the way you think about things?

- **Decide if you really should feel angry**

Are you an angry person who seems to get mad too often or without good reason? When angry, ask yourself if the facts of the situation warrant an angry reaction on your part. Or, ask yourself if your anger is the result of a character defect (i.e., you get mad frequently for little things).

- **Identify the effects of your anger and your methods of coping with anger**

How does your anger and your methods of coping affect your physical, mental, or spiritual health? How are your relationships with family members, friends, or others affected?

■ **Use different strategies to deal with anger**

These include cognitive (your beliefs about anger and the internal messages you give yourself), behavioral (how you act), and verbal (what you say to other people) strategies. Having a variety of strategies puts you in a good position to cope with anger in a wide range of situations.

■ **Cognitive strategies for anger management**

Evaluate your beliefs about anger and change those beliefs that cause you problems. For example, if you believe you should "let it out" every time you get angry, you may find this isn't always the best policy and this belief should be modified. Or, if you believe you should never get mad, you might have to change this belief and give yourself permission to feel anger.

- Catch yourself when you are angry and change your angry thoughts.

- Determine if your anger is really justified given the situation. This requires not jumping to conclusions and getting all the facts of the situation first.

- Use positive self-talk or slogans (for example, "This too will pass;" "Keep your cool and stay in control," etc.).

- Use fantasy. Imagine yourself coping in a positive way.

- Evaluate the risks and benefits of expressing your anger or holding it inside.

- Remind yourself of the negative effects of ignoring anger and holding it inside.

- Remind yourself of the negative effects of expressing anger towards others in hurtful ways.

- Identify the benefits of handling anger in a positive way.

- Take a few minutes at the end of the day to see if you are harboring any anger from the day's events.

■ **Verbal strategies for anger management**

- Express your anger to the person you're upset with.

- Discuss the situation or problem that contributed to your anger directly to the person with whom you are angry.

- Share your angry feelings with a friend, family member, therapist, AA, NA, or CA sponsor. Many find it helpful to discuss anger at support group meetings.

- Discuss the situation or problem that contributed to your anger with a neutral person to get their opinion on the situation.

- Apologize or make amends to others who were hurt as a result of how you expressed your anger.

■ **Behavior strategies for anger management**

Direct angry energy towards physical activity such as walking, exercise, or sports.

- Direct feelings of anger towards some type of work.

- Express your anger with creative media such as painting, drawing, and other forms of arts and crafts.

- Write about your feelings in a journal or anger log.

- Practice verbal strategies mentioned in the previous section to better prepare yourself to express your feelings to others.

- Use reminder cards that provide specific coping strategies you can use to deal with anger.

- Leave situations in which your anger is so intense you might lose control and do something irrational or violent.

SETTING A GOAL

My **goal** in relation to how I cope with my anger is:

_____

_____

_____

Steps I will take to reach this goal are:

_____

_____

_____

Potential benefits of reaching my goal are:

_____

_____

_____

Seek professional help if you experience serious problems as a result of anger, how you cope with it or your inability to gain better control of it on your own. Professional help is especially important for those who act out angry impulses by hitting or hurting others or breaking objects. Professional treatment also can help those who turn anger against themselves and exhibit self-destructive tendencies such as those who cut, burn, or hurt themselves.

4
Anxiety and Worry

Most people feel anxious and worry from time to time. However, some people experience excessive anxiety and worry to the point where their lives are impaired. Many rely on alcohol or drugs to decrease their symptoms only to find in the long run such use can lead to chemical dependency.

Anxiety and worry are closely related. Anxiety refers to the *physical* side and worry refers to the *mental* side. When you have one, you usually have the other.

Some of the ways in which anxiety shows include shortness of breath, rapid heart beat, tightness or discomfort in the chest, feeling lightheaded or weak, feeling uptight or on edge, tingling or numbness.

Anticipatory anxiety refers to feelings of anxiety associated with thinking ahead of time and what "may happen" in the future. Another term used to describe this is *fear of anxiety.* Some people avoid situations because of their fear of anxiety. Examples of places or situations commonly avoided include shopping in a large or crowded store or standing in check-out lines; attending church; going to the doctor or dentist; going to movies, sporting events, or music concerts; driving through tunnels or over bridges; riding elevators or escalators; or traveling by plane, bus, or train. In some cases, people become so anxious and fearful of leaving home that they seldom or never leave their home.

Worry refers to thinking about something over and over in your head. Worry may occur in relation to a *real* problem, or it may occur in relation to a *potential* problem — something that you think is likely to happen. People who worry a lot often feel inadequate in coping with the problems or situations they worry about. Some of the things people worry a lot about include their health or the health of other family members, making correct decisions and doing what's right, being on time, losing control of feelings or behaviors, pleasing and making other people happy, and staying sober or clean.

The questions that follow will help you clarify where you stand in relation to anxiety and worry.

1. On a scale of one to 10, how much of a problem is your anxiety and/or worry, or how you cope with these (✓ your rating)?

1	3	5	7	10
No Problem	Moderate Problem	Significant Problem	Serious Problem	Severe Problem

_____ _____ _____ _____ _____

Put your rating here for your *anxiety* _____.

Put your rating here for your *worry* _____.

If your ratings were three or higher for either of these, you should consider seeking professional help. If your ratings were five or higher, you should definitely seek professional help with a mental health specialist.

2. My anxiety shows in the following ways:

_____

_____

_____

3. I get anxious because:

_____

_____

_____

4. My anxiety and worry has affected my life in the following ways:

_____

_____

_____

_____

5. My anxiety and worry has affected my relationships in the following ways:

_____

_____

_____

_____

6. I worry a lot about:

_____

_____

_____

_____

7. The things I feel anxious or worry about that actually happen (and how often?):

_____

_____

_____

_____

_____

8. The connection between my use of alcohol or other drugs and my anxiety or worry is:

_____

_____

_____

_____

COPING WITH ANXIETY AND WORRY

■ **Identify and label anxiety and worry**

Know the signs and symptoms of excessive anxiety or worry. This will help you "catch" yourself when you feel anxious or are worrying too much.

■ **Find out what is causing your anxiety and worry**

Identify the specific problems, situations, or things that cause you to feel anxious and worried. If these are *real* problems, look at ways to solve these. If these are *potential* problems ask yourself if these problems will really occur. Work on changing how you think about potential problems.

■ **Get a physical examination**

This will help to determine if medical problems are contributing to your anxiety.

■ **Evaluate your diet**

Take a close look at what you are eating or taking into your body. Try to figure out if your use of caffeine, sugar, or other foods are contributing to anxiety and making you feel on edge.

■ **Evaluate your lifestyle**

Make sure that you are getting enough rest, relaxation, and exercise. Exercise can help release some of your anxious feelings and may serve the additional benefit of helping to prevent anxious feelings from building up.

■ **Meditate**

Meditation can help you feel calmer and gain better control over your anxiety.

■ **Learn relaxation techniques**

There are many books and tapes available that can help you teach yourself relaxation. Or, you can learn relaxation techniques from a professional therapist.

■ **Practice proper breathing techniques**

Stop shallow or rapid breathing or holding your breatn. Learn proper ways of breathing and practice these each day until they become automatic. You can practice breathing techniques anywhere — at work, home, in the car, before a speech, or before going into a situation about which you feel anxious.

■ **Change your beliefs or thoughts**

Practice changing your "anxious" and "worrisome" thoughts or beliefs. When working on a *real* problem causing your anxiety or worry, view the problem for what it is. Don't look at it as a barrier you can't overcome. When feeling overly anxious or worried about a *potential* problem, ask yourself what evidence you have that the problem will ever occur or what you fear about the outcome. Try to identify all possible outcomes, not just the negative ones, that you worry might happen. Make positive "self" statements such as, "I can do it," "My anxiety won't get the best of me," "I'm in control of my worry," "It's OK to make mistakes," or "No one has to be perfect."

■ **Share your anxious feelings and thoughts with others**

Discussing your feelings and worries with a friend, family member, sponsor, or counselor may help you feel better and gain relief. This can also help you learn what others do to handle their anxiety and/or worry and identify new ways to cope. However, keep in mind that you can overwhelm others if you constantly share your worries. Sharing your feelings without making attempts at getting better might turn others off. People usually don't mind hearing their friends' or loved ones' feelings unless the same old story is told over and over.

■ **Set aside "worry" time each day**

Try to avoid worrying throughout the day and save your worries for a specific time you call your "worry time." Pick a place and regular time, then allow yourself to let your worries out. Don't go on endlessly and limit yourself to no more than one-half hour a day for this worry time.

■ **Keep a written anxiety-and-worry journal**

Writing your thoughts and feelings in a journal will help you better understand and release your thoughts and feelings. This can also help you identify patterns of your anxiety and worry, coping strategies that don't work, and coping strategies that work in reducing anxiety and worry. This can also help you track your progress over time.

■ **Face the situations causing you to feel anxious and worry**

Reality is often not as bad as what you think it might be. When you directly face situations you find difficult, your confidence level should increase. Start with the least threatening anxiety- or worry-provoking situations and gradually build towards facing the more difficult ones. Engaging in situations you feel anxious and worry about should reduce your anxiety and worry.

■ **If your anxiety level continues to cause you significant distress, consult a mental health professional**

A consultation with a mental health professional (psychiatrist, psychologist, social worker, counselor, etc.) will help you determine if your anxiety is a symptom of a psychiatric illness. Many treatments are available to help individuals with anxiety disorders. These include different types of psychotherapy as well as medication. Be careful about types of medication used as it is easy to become dependent on medications such as tranquilizers. Let your doctor know that you are recovering from a chemical dependency so that the proper medications are used should your symptoms be serious enough to require the use of medicine.

SETTING A GOAL

My **goal** in relation to my anxiety and/or worry is:

_____

_____

_____

Steps I will take to reach this goal are:

_____

_____

_____

Potential benefits of reaching my goal are:

_____

_____

_____

5
Boredom

Feelings of boredom lead some people back to alcohol or other drugs. If your lifestyle was wrapped up in alcohol or drugs, or in the "fast life," being clean or sober may feel boring at first. You may even miss the "action" more than you miss alcohol or drugs.

Replacing drug and alcohol activities with new ones takes time and effort. You have to guard against letting boredom serve as an excuse to use chemicals again. Perhaps you gave up some of your non-drug and alcohol interests over time as your addiction took over your life.

You may also feel bored with your job, your relationships, or other life circumstances. Chemical use may have covered up your boredom and unhappiness. Now, you have to face these issues. If you are bored with your life try to figure out why. For example, perhaps you are bored in your relationship because your needs aren't being met. Or, maybe you are bored at work because you aren't able to use your talents or your job isn't challenging.

Answer the following questions to help you clarify where you stand in relation to boredom and to more clearly see how your addiction may have contributed to it.

1. On a scale of one to 10, how much of a problem is your boredom or how you cope with it (✓ your rating)?

1	3	5	7	10
No Problem	Moderate Problem	Significant Problem	Serious Problem	Severe Problem
_____	_____	_____	_____	_____

If you wrote down a rating of three or more, it is recommended that you learn new ways of dealing with boredom. If you wrote down a rating of five or more, it is recommended that you consider therapy if you are not already in treatment.

2. I enjoy the following hobbies or activities:

_____

_____

_____

_____

3. As a result of my chemical dependency I gave up these activities:

    _____

    _____

    _____

    _____

4. Of this list, I miss the following activities the most:

    _____

    _____

    _____

    _____

5. I would like to get involved in these activities again:

    _____

    _____

    _____

    _____

6. New activities or interests that I could get involved in include:

    _____

    _____

    _____

7. Are you easily bored? ☐ Yes ☐ No   Explain your answer.

_____

_____

_____

_____

8. What excites me and makes me feel good about life is:

_____

_____

_____

_____

COPING WITH BOREDOM

■ Recognize your boredom and determine the reasons

Everybody feels bored now and then. But for alcoholics and drug addicts, it can represent a threat to relapse. Pay attention to times when you feel bored and figure out why you feel this way.

■ Regain "lost" activities

Get involved in activities that you enjoyed prior to your chemical dependency. Figure out what used to bring you pleasure and fun that didn't involve alcohol or drug use.

■ Learn to appreciate the simple pleasures in life

If you have a need for high levels of action, excitement, and risk, you have to learn to enjoy simple, day-to-day pleasures. Don't expect to always be able to satisfy your need for "action." Give yourself time to learn how to enjoy the simple pleasures in life such as quiet time alone, talking with a friend or loved one, reading a magazine, or taking a walk.

■ **Develop new interests**

Learn new hobbies, develop new interests, or find new forms of pleasure or enjoyment. Think about activities or hobbies that you always wanted to do. Choose one and make plans to do it.

■ **Build fun into your day-to-day life**

You may wish to complete a daily or weekly list of pleasant activities to make sure you have fun. Try to find a balance of fun activities involving other people and those involving just yourself. Do something fun or enjoyable at least once a day.

■ **Identify "high-risk" times for feeling bored**

For many people recovering from chemical dependency, evenings and weekends are the times where they are most likely to feel bored. These often were the times during which they used alcohol or other drugs. Knowing your high-risk times puts you in a position to plan recovery or social activities during these times.

■ **Change your thoughts about boredom**

Expect some boredom and don't think you always have to be busy at something. Lower your expectations if needed. And don't expect others to be responsible for making your boredom go away. It's up to you. Boredom can be a signal that something in your relationships or lifestyle needs to change. Challenge thoughts such as, "I'm bored, I need alcohol or drugs."

■ **Carefully evaluate relationship or job boredom before making any major changes**

If you are having serious problems feeling bored in a close relationship or your job, figure out why and what you need to do. Perhaps you need to work on improving, ending, or finding new relationships. Or, maybe you need a change in your job or job responsibilities. However, major changes in relationships, jobs, or other major areas of life should be well thought through. In the early months of recovery, be careful of making major changes too quickly, such as developing a new romantic relationship. Many have relapsed because a new relationship became more important than their recovery.

■ Deal with persistent feelings of boredom

If you persistently feel bored, this may be a sign that you have a psychiatric illness. If you feel very empty inside and nothing seems to have meaning or purpose in your life, consult a professional mental health therapist. You can benefit from therapy. In a later section of this workbook, information will be provided on dealing with emptiness and joylessness. These are often closely associated with persistent feelings of boredom.

■ Participate in support groups

Attending meetings of self-help programs (AA, NA, CA, or mental health support groups) will help you keep busy and meet new people. Many self-help programs sponsor social activities such as dances, skating parties, picnics, bowling, or organized trips to ball games. In some areas, there are "recovery clubs" which provide an opportunity to socialize without the threat of alcohol or drugs. Recovery clubs also sponsor social events. Any of these activities can help you cope with boredom in addition to offering other benefits.

SETTING A GOAL

My **goal** in relation to my boredom is:

_____

_____

_____

Steps I will take to reach this goal are:

_____

_____

_____

Potential benefits of reaching my goal are:

_____

_____

_____

6
Depression

Depression is closely associated with chemical dependency. Drugs such as alcohol, opiates, tranquilizers, and sedatives depress the central nervous system and can cause you to feel depressed. Depression is also associated with "crashing" from the effects of cocaine or other stimulant drugs.

Problems and losses caused by chemical dependency also contribute to feelings of depression. Many things are lost because of alcohol and drugs — relationships, jobs, status, health, money, dignity, and self-esteem.

Sometimes depression is caused by a relapse to chemical use, especially after a significant period of abstinence.

Getting sober or clean, and staying sober and clean, often helps decrease or eliminate feelings of depression for many chemically dependent people. However, this is not always the case. You may still feel depressed even if you've been sober or clean for weeks or months. Or, you may experience depression long after you're sober or clean.

Some people have a type of depression that goes beyond the blues or feeling down that we all experience from time to time. This is referred to as *Clinical Depression* and requires professional treatment. Chemically dependent people have higher rates of clinical depression than the general population.

Clinical depression involves feeling depressed or being unable to experience pleasure for several weeks or longer. Other depressive symptoms include loss of appetite; decrease in sexual desire or energy; difficulty concentrating; significant weight change; problems falling asleep, staying asleep, or sleeping too much; feeling agitated or restless; feeling hopeless, helpless, worthless, or guilty; even feeling like life is not worth living; or making an actual attempt at suicide. For some people, symptoms have been more or less present for months and months, or even longer.

Even if you don't have a clinical depression it still can help to learn some new ways to handle feelings of depression so that your recovery goes better. Following are some questions to help you assess your depression.

1. I have experienced the following symptoms for this long: (Use a 10-point scale when determining "to what degree" you are experiencing a specific symptom with 1 – not at all, 5 – to a significant degree, 10 – to a serious degree.)

Symptom	To What Degree (1-10)?	How Long?
◆ Feeling depressed or sad	_____	_____
◆ Trouble experiencing pleasure	_____	_____
◆ Appetite disturbance	_____	_____
◆ Sleep disturbance	_____	_____
◆ Feeling agitated or irritable	_____	_____
◆ Feeling slowed down	_____	_____
◆ Difficulty concentrating or remembering things	_____	_____
◆ Feeling helpless, hopeless, or guilty	_____	_____
◆ Loss or decrease in sexual desire	_____	_____
◆ Thoughts of taking life	_____	_____
◆ Plan to take your life	_____	_____
◆ Actual suicide attempt	_____	_____

2. On a scale of one to 10, how much of a problem is depression for you (✓ your rating)?

1	3	5	7	10
No Problem	Moderate Problem	Significant Problem	Serious Problem	Severe Problem
_____	_____	_____	_____	_____

If your rating was three or higher, you should consider talking with a professional to determine if you need treatment. If your rating was five or higher, you should definitely seek professional help. If you have strong thoughts of taking your life, an actual plan, or have made an attempt, call a mental health professional now.

3. Depression has affected my life in the following ways:

_____

_____

_____

_____

4. I am currently depressed because:

    _____

    _____

    _____

    _____

5. I tend to have a lot of negative, pessimistic, or depressing thoughts (for example, always thinking about the worse-case scenario, seeing only the negative side of situations, exaggerating problems, or making mountains out of molehills, etc.).

    ❑ Yes   ❑ No

    Explain your answer.

    _____

    _____

    _____

6. My use of alcohol or drugs and my depression are connected in the following ways:

    _____

    _____

    _____

    _____

COPING WITH DEPRESSION

■ **Find out the problems causing your depression and do something about them**

Solving problems contributing to depression should help you feel better. If you feel depressed because you are overweight, then do something about your weight. If you feel depressed because you hate your job, look at other options. If you feel depressed because your relationships are unsatisfying, look for ways to improve these relationships or develop new ones.

However, depression is not always related to "problems" or "life events." Sometimes, biological factors may be the primary factor contributing to depression. This is especially true of people who have two or more episodes of clinical depression, called *Recurrent Depression,* and with this type of depression your chances of having future episodes are increased.

Make sure you get a thorough physical examination so that medical causes of depression can be ruled out first.

■ Evaluate your relationships with other people

Develop new relationships or improve relationships that are problematic and contribute to your feeling depressed. Look at whether your current relationships are satisfying your emotional needs.

■ Make amends

Depression can be connected to guilt associated with hurting others because of your chemical dependency. Making amends can help you feel less depressed and better about yourself. The AA and NA 12-Step Programs can help guide you through the process. A counselor or sponsor can help you determine when you are ready to face specific individuals whom you feel were hurt by your chemical use.

■ Keep active

Even if you have to force yourself to do things, keep active in your social relationships, and with your hobbies and interests. When you least want to do things may be when you most need to. Physical activity like walking, running, working out, working around the house or yard, or playing sports may indirectly help improve your depression.

■ Talk about your feelings and problems with others

Share your feelings of sadness or depression with supportive people such as close friends or family members. Talk about your feelings with your sponsor or a counselor.

Venting your feelings may provide some relief and help you gain a different perspective on your depression. Or, you may learn some new ways of coping with depression from other people.

However, you must guard against always talking about your feelings with others. People are usually supportive to a degree. If you don't try to help yourself and do some things differently to cope with your depression, others can get tired of hearing you constantly talk about your depressed feelings.

■ Look for other feelings that may contribute to, or be associated with, depression

Other emotions may contribute to feelings of depression. Some people are prone to feeling more depressed when they suppress or hold onto feelings of anger. Others who feel guilty and shameful may be prone to depression if they don't figure out ways to work through these feelings. Some people get depressed as a result of constantly feeling anxious or fearful.

■ Change your depressed thoughts

Your thoughts can contribute to feelings of depression. Learn to identify and challenge negative, pessimistic, or depressed thoughts. Avoid making mountains out of molehills, always looking at the negative side of things, always expecting the worse case scenario, or dwelling on your mistakes or shortcomings.

You can use self-talk strategies to change negative thoughts. (For example, in response to making a mistake, instead of saying, "I'm not capable of doing this;" say, "I made a mistake. It's no big deal, everyone makes mistakes.")

■ Focus on positive things

Make sure you acknowledge your positive points or strengths. Don't take yourself for granted and give yourself credit for your positive qualities.

Take an inventory of your achievements or the positive things happening in your life, no matter how small. Learn to look at the "other" side of things when you catch yourself thinking negatively. For example, suppose you lost 25 pounds over several months only to gain five back. Rather than put yourself down and feel depressed for gaining five pounds back, remind yourself that you still are 20 pounds less than your previous weight. Remember, sometimes it's not so much what you do but how you think about what you do that determines how you feel.

■ **Keep a journal**

Writing about your feelings can help you release them, better understand them, and help you to figure out if there are patterns to your feelings and behaviors. For example, suppose you discover that you always tend to feel more depressed after visiting your parents. In exploring this further, you discover these feelings relate to constantly being criticized by your father, or because your mother is usually drunk when you visit, which triggers bad feelings and memories from the past. A journal can also help you keep track of changes in your depression over time as well as positive coping strategies that seem to help you the most. In addition, you can write about positive or hopeful things that happen to you each day.

■ **Participate in pleasant activities each day**

Put some time aside each day to do something that is fun, enjoyable, or pleasurable. It doesn't matter how small this is. Even little things like taking 15 minutes each day to read a magazine and enjoy a cup of coffee or tea may help you feel better.

■ **Identify and plan enjoyable future activities**

We all need things to look forward to; whether it is buying something nice for ourselves, taking a vacation, or participating in an enjoyable activity. Looking forward breaks up the monotony of doing the same old things over and over. It provides a focus for your energy and can make you feel invested in life. Set some goals in relation to activities, events, or experiences that you can plan and look forward to.

■ **If your depression doesn't get better, seek an evaluation by a mental health professional**

If these or other coping techniques don't seem to help much, and your depression continues and causes you personal suffering or interferes with your life, seek an evaluation with a mental health professional. There are many different types of treatment effective for clinical depression including various types of therapy as well as the use of antidepressant medications. Not all clinical depressions need medications. But if yours does, you should not feel guilty. It is not the same as drinking alcohol or using drugs to get high or loaded.

For many people, clinical depression is a lifelong disorder requiring ongoing treatment. If you have had two or more episodes of serious depression you probably need ongoing treatment, even after your depression improves or lifts completely. People who stop treatment for depression put themselves at risk for relapse in the future.

SETTING A GOAL

My **goal** in relation to my depression is:

_____

_____

_____

Steps I will take to reach this goal are:

_____

_____

_____

Potential benefits of reaching my goal are:

_____

_____

_____

7
Feeling Empty or Joyless

When you stop using alcohol and other drugs, you may feel "empty" and it may be difficult to feel joy or pleasure. You may believe your life lacks meaning or purpose and feel miserable as a result. If such feelings continue for months into your recovery, it places you at risk for relapse, and reverting to chemical use will seem like a better option than feeling empty and lacking joy.

Negative consequences of your chemical dependency contribute to these feelings. Some people seem to lose their capacity to experience joy as their addictions progress.

The following statements will help you assess where you stand in relation to feeling empty or joyless; next are suggestions on how to cope with these feelings.

1.   On a scale of one to 10, rate the degree to which you currently feel empty; you feel your life lacks meaning, purpose, or direction (✓ your rating).

1	3	5	7	10
No Emptiness	Moderate Degree of Emptiness	Good Deal of Emptiness	Great Deal of Emptiness	Tremendous Degree of Emptiness
_____	_____	_____	_____	_____

2.   On a scale of one to 10, rate the degree to which you currently feel problems experiencing joy in your daily life (✓ your rating).

1	3	5	7	10
No Problem	Moderate Degree of Joylessness	Good Deal of Joylessness	Great Deal of Joylessness	Tremendous Degree of Joylessness
_____	_____	_____	_____	_____

If you rated yourself three or higher to either of the preceding statements, it is recommended that you begin to learn ways to find meaning in your life. If you rated yourself five or higher you should seek therapy if not already involved in treatment with a professional.

3.   I feel empty or joyless because:

_____

_____

_____

_____

4. Most important in my life is (for example, a good family life, close friends, success, being creative, being kind and loving, helping other people, being at peace with God or myself, etc.):

_____

_____

_____

_____

5. What makes me feel good about myself or brings me a sense of purpose and satisfaction is:

_____

_____

_____

_____

6. I (have or do not have) close relationships with others. Explain your answer.

_____

_____

_____

_____

7. I feel like I (am, am not) using my talents, abilities, or creativity (at work, at home, in your social life, etc.). Explain your answer.

_____

_____

_____

_____

8. My use of alcohol or other drugs affected my feeling empty or joyless by:

_____

_____

_____

_____

9. I (do or do not) feel connected to God or a Higher Power. Explain your answer.

_____

_____

_____

_____

COPING WITH EMPTINESS

■ **Nurture your relationships**

Sharing quality time with family and friends who are important to you is one of the best ways you can cope with feeling empty or joyless. Showing concern, expressing love, spending time with, and taking an interest in other people is a good way to nurture relationships.

■ **Be of service to others**

Helping others can bring you meaning and purpose. There are many things you can do to help out a friend, family member, or fellow AA/NA member. You can be of service to others by helping out at AA/NA meetings and volunteering on community, church, school committees, or task groups. When you are well grounded in recovery, you can be of service to others by serving as a sponsor. In the meantime, providing rides to meetings and showing support to fellow AA's or NA's is a good way to be of service to others.

■ **Get involved in the spiritual aspect of recovery**

Developing a relationship with God or a Higher Power is one of the key ways of feeling a sense of meaning in life. Praying, reading the Bible, or communicating with your Higher Power in your own personal way helps you to develop your spirituality. You may also benefit from attending services at your church, synagogue, or other place of worship.

■ Focus on important activities

Figure out the work or leisure activities which bring you a sense of joy or pleasure and spend time in these activities. Develop hobbies and interests that excite you and give you something to look forward to.

■ Focus on your achievements

Give yourself credit for your achievements related to your recovery, work, hobbies, creative, or athletic activities.

■ Attend support group meetings

Attending support group meetings provides you with a chance to get close to others, work your recovery program, and focus on spirituality.

■ Use the 12-Step Program

Working the 12 steps helps you to develop your spirituality in recovery. Many of the 12 steps provide a way to rely on your Higher Power and to seek forgiveness for things you've done in your addiction that hurt you or others.

■ Set goals for the future

Setting goals gives you something to work towards. Goals help you structure your time and provide a way to measure your progress. It is helpful to have short-term goals (less than three months), medium-range goals (three to six months) and long-term goals (more than six months).

■ Build structure in your life

Having things to do and structuring your days and weeks will prevent you from aimlessly going about your life. Even if you are not currently working and have a lot of time on your hands you can build structure by using a daily and weekly schedule.

■ Change your thoughts about excitement

If you believe that you can't feel much pleasure or joy in life unless you are "living on the edge" and involved in dangerous activities, change your thought process. You may have to learn to enjoy the simple pleasures in life that don't involve "action" all of the time. If you consider yourself an "action junkie" you will need to decrease your need for constant action and excitement, and slowly learn to enjoy routine aspects of life. Tell yourself that "living on the edge" caused you more trouble than it was worth.

SETTING A GOAL

My **goal** in relation to feeling empty or lacking joy in my life is:

_____

_____

_____

Steps I will take to reach this goal are:

_____

_____

_____

Potential benefits of reaching my goal are:

_____

_____

_____

_____

8
Guilt and Shame

Feeling guilty and shameful are closely associated with chemical dependency.

Guilt refers to "feeling bad" about your behaviors. You can feel guilty for things that you have done as well as things that you have not done or failed to do. For example, you may feel guilty for using family income for chemicals; hurting, lying and conning family or friends; or breaking laws in order to get money to pay for drugs. Or, you may feel guilty for not fulfilling your obligations or your responsibilities with your family. Perhaps this showed by not spending time or taking much interest in the lives of your parents, spouse, or children.

Shame refers to "feeling bad about yourself." You feel weak, defective, or like you are a failure. When you feel shameful, you feel something is wrong with *you*.

Like many of the other recovery tasks, it will take time and effort to work through guilt and shame. Complete the following statements to help you clarify where you stand in relation to guilt and shame to get you started in creating an action plan.

GUILT

1. Behaviors or actions on my part during my chemical use that I feel guilty about include:

    _____

    _____

    _____

    _____

2. Of these behaviors, the two I feel the most guilt about are:

    _____

    _____

    _____

    _____

3. Some things that I failed to do during my chemical use for which I feel guilty include (for example, not spending time with your family, not fulfilling work, school or financial obligations, etc.):

_____

_____

_____

_____

4. Of these behaviors, the two I feel the most guilt about are:

_____

_____

_____

_____

5. Now go back and carefully review your answers. On a scale of one to 10, how much *guilt* do you feel regarding what you did or failed to do because of your chemical dependency (✓ your rating)?

1	3	5	7	10
No Guilt	Moderate Degree of Guilt	Good Deal of Guilt	Great Deal of Guilt	Tremendous Degree of Guilt
_____	_____	_____	_____	_____

If you rated yourself three or higher, it is recommended that you begin dealing with your feelings of guilt. If you rated yourself five or higher you should consider therapy if you are not already in treatment.

SHAME

1. My feelings of shame are:

_____

_____

_____

_____

2. My chemical dependency changed me in the following ways:

_____

_____

_____

3. The people in whose presence I feel the most shame are:

_____

_____

_____

_____

4. On a scale of one to 10, how would you rate yourself in terms of the degree to which you feel *shameful* about yourself because of your chemical dependency and what it's done to your life (✓ your rating)?

1	3	5	7	10
No Shame	Moderate Amount of Shame	Good Deal of Shame	Great Deal of Shame	Tremendous Degree of Shame
_____	_____	_____	_____	_____

If you rated yourself three or higher, it is recommended that you begin dealing with your feelings of shame. If you rated yourself five or higher you may wish to consider therapy if you are not already in treatment.

COPING WITH GUILT AND SHAME

■ **Recognize your guilt and shame**

Be honest with yourself about what you did or failed to do as a result of your chemical use, and how you feel about yourself. Completing the previous section was a great way to begin this step.

■ **Give yourself time to feel better about yourself**

Be realistic in terms of accepting the reality that it may take a good deal of time to feel less guilt and less shame. Change may come initially in small steps such as feeling a little less guilty now than in the past. Remember, feeling better about yourself will be connected to making positive changes in yourself and your lifestyle.

■ **Accept your limitations**

Admit and accept your flaws and limitations. Don't blame yourself for having an addictive disease. Instead, take responsibility to make positive change by becoming sober and clean, staying sober and clean, and dealing directly with problems caused by your chemical dependency.

■ **Share your feelings of guilt and shame**

Talk with others about your feelings of guilt and shame. Share your true feelings and admit honestly the things you did that hurt others as a result of your chemical dependency. The intimate details of your actions or inactions are best shared with someone who understands chemical dependency (such as a therapist, sponsor, or clergy member.)

■ **Use the 12-step Program**

Use the 12 steps of AA, NA, and CA. Many of these steps directly and indirectly help with guilt and shame feelings. For example, Step Five states *"admitted to God, to ourselves, and to another human being, the exact nature of our wrongs."*

■ **Make amends**

Make amends to others who were hurt by your chemical dependency. This puts you in a better position to receive forgiveness from others. The 12-Step Program of AA, NA, or CA can help guide you through this process.

■ **Seek forgiveness**

You can directly ask for forgiveness from those who were hurt by your chemical dependency. Keep in mind that the risk you take is that some people may not wish to forgive you for what you've done to hurt them. Also, asking forgiveness must be done with sincerity; you must accept that it will be meaningless unless you work hard at your recovery and show positive changes in your behaviors. You can also ask forgiveness from God or a Higher Power.

SETTING A GOAL

My **goal** in relation to my guilt and/or shame is:

_____

_____

_____

Steps I will take to reach this goal are:

_____

_____

_____

Potential benefits of reaching my goal are:

_____

_____

_____

9
Love and Recovery

We all need love in our lives. Feeling loved and cared about, and loving and caring about other people, makes us happy. Having loving relationships with others is one of the most basic of all human needs. Such relationships enrich our lives.

On the other hand, a lack of loving relationships, an inability to express or show love towards others, or an inability to actually feel love towards others causes you to feel bad, depressed, lonely, or empty. Chemical dependency hurts love relationships. Recovery, on the other hand, provides chances to restore loving relationships and develop new ones.

Although you may think about love as simply a feeling or emotion, it is much more. It is also an attitude and approach to others and to life. Love involves your behaviors or what you say and do. With love, similar to other feelings, actions speak louder than words. How you treat others reveals your feelings more than what you say to them. For instance, you could tell another person how much you care about and love them but treat them shabbily. Or, you may seldom tell another that you love or care for them, but treat them with much kindness, respect, and love in your actions.

The following statements will help you assess how much love is in your life at the current time.

1. On a scale of one to 10, rate how much love you feel you get from others (✓ your rating).

1	3	5	7	10
Very Little Love	Moderate Amount of Love	Good Deal of Love	Great Deal of Love	Tremendous Degree of Love
_____	_____	_____	_____	_____

2. On a scale of one to 10, rate how much love you feel you give to others (✓ your rating).

1	3	5	7	10
Very Little Love	Moderate Amount of Love	Good Deal of Love	Great Deal of Love	Tremendous Degree of Love
_____	_____	_____	_____	_____

3. My chemical dependency affected my ability to care about or show love towards other people in the following ways:

_____

_____

_____

4. I (am or am not) "getting" enough love from others in my life:

_____

_____

_____

5. I (am or am not) "giving" enough love to others in my life:

_____

_____

_____

6. I usually express or show my love towards the following people in these ways:

   • My parent(s) or caretaker(s)

_____

_____

   • My spouse or partner

_____

_____

   • My brothers or sisters

_____

_____

- My children

_____

_____

- My grandchildren

_____

_____

- My close friends

_____

_____

- Other people

_____

_____

7. Others would describe my ability to show love in my actions or behavior in this way:

_____

_____

_____

_____

SETTING A GOAL

My **goal** in relation to expressing love or improving my love relationships is:

_____

_____

_____

Steps I will take to reach this goal are:

_____

_____

_____

Potential benefits of reaching my goal are:

_____

_____

_____

10
Expressing Positive Feelings

In the previous sections, much attention was directed towards "negative feelings" such as anger, anxiety, depression, emptiness, guilt, etc. However, feelings also have a "positive" aspect. For instance, anger can motivate you to resolve problems, differences, and conflicts with others. Or, anger can motivate you to work hard at reaching your goals and achieving positive things in life.

Much emphasis was also placed on being able to handle a variety of "negative" emotional states in order to reduce the chances of a relapse, make you feel better about yourself and make your life more satisfying. It is just as important to be aware of, and express, "positive" feelings. Expressing positive feelings such as affection, love, joy, and happiness can bring you closer to others and improve your relationships. Ideally, there should be a balance in your life in expressing a range of feelings.

The questions that follow will help you focus on your experiences in relation to positive emotional states.

1. On a scale of one to 10, how able are you to express your positive emotions towards others (✓ your rating)?

1	3	5	7	10
	Fairly Easy to	Somewhat Difficult	Very Difficult	Extremely Difficult
Easy to Express	Express Positive	to Express	to Express	to Express
Positive Feelings	Feelings	Positive Feelings	Positive Feelings	Positive Feelings
_____	_____	_____	_____	_____

If you gave yourself a rating of five or above you should consider learning how to express your positive feelings to others.

2. Positive feelings that are the easiest for me to express include:

_____

_____

_____

3.   Positive feelings that are the most difficult for me to express include:

_____

_____

_____

4.   The last time I shared a positive feeling with each of the following people was:

- My spouse or partner   _____
- My mother or father   _____
- My son or daughter   _____
- My brother or sister   _____
- Other relative   _____
- A close friend   _____

5.   Sharing positive feelings with others can benefit my relationships in the following ways:

_____

_____

_____

SETTING A GOAL

My **goal** in relation to expressing positive feelings is:

_____

_____

_____

Steps I will take to reach this goal are:

_____

_____

_____

Potential benefits of reaching my goal are:

_____

_____

_____

APPENDIX A
COPING WITH FEELINGS WORKSHEET

1. Write a brief description of the situation or event that caused you to experience an upset feeling or emotion.

    _____

    _____

    _____

2. List the feelings or emotions this experience triggered.

    _____

    _____

3. List your specific thoughts in relation to this situation and the upset feeling you experienced.

    _____

    _____

4. Describe how you coped with this upset feeling. How did you act or what did you do?

    _____

    _____

5. New Coping Strategies:

    A. List some *new thoughts* regarding this situation and your upset feeling.

    _____

    _____

    B. List some *new behaviors or actions* to help you cope with this feeling.

    _____

    _____

APPENDIX B
SUGGESTED READINGS

📖 Agras, S. *Facing Fears, Phobias, and Anxiety.* New York: Freeman, 1985.

📖 Bourne, E. *The Anxiety and Phobia Workbook.* Oakland, CA: New Harbinger Publications, Inc., 1990.

📖 Burns, D. *Feeling Good: The New Mood Therapy.* New York: William Morrow and Company, 1980.

📖 ———. *The Feeling Good Handbook.* New York: William Morrow and Company, 1990.

📖 Club, G.A. *Coping with Panic.* Belmond, CA: Brooks/Cole, 1990.

📖 Daley, D. *Kicking Addictive Habits Once and For All: A Relapse Prevention Guide.* Lexington, MA: Lexington Press, 1991.

📖 ———. *Coping with Anger Workbook.* Skokie, IL: Gerald T. Rogers Productions, Inc., 1992.

📖 Glanz, L. *Overcoming Anxiety and Worry.* Skokie, IL: Gerald T. Rogers Productions, Inc., 1991.

📖 Goodwin, D.W. *Anxiety.* New York: Oxford University Press, 1986.

📖 Jeffers, S. *Feel the Fear and Do It Anyway.* New York: Fawcett Columbine, 1987.

📖 Lerner, H. *The Dance of Anger.* New York: Harper and Row, 1985.

📖 Lewinsohn, P., R. Munoz, M. Youngren, and A. Zeiss. *Control Your Depression.* New York: Prentice Hall, 1986.

📖 Papolos, D., and J. Papolos. *Overcoming Depression.* New York: Harper and Row, 1987.

📖 Rosellini, G., and M. Worden. *Here Comes the Sun.* Center City, MN: Hazelden, 1987.

📖 Seagrave, A., and F. Covington. *Free From Fears: New Help for Anxiety, Panic and Agoraphobia.* New York: Poseidon Press, 1987.,

📖 Sheehan, D. *The Anxiety Disease.* New York: Charles Schribner and Sons, 1984.

📖 Tauris, C. *Anger: The Misunderstood Emotion,* 2nd ed. New York: Simon and Schuster, Inc., 1989.

📖 Weekes, C. *More Help for Your Nerves.* New York: Bantam Books, 1984.